W9-BFD-500

Living History

Pioneer Farm

Living on a Farm in the 1880s

by Megan O'Hara
Photography by Tim Rummelhoff

Content Consultant
Jim Mattson, Site Manager
Oliver Kelley Farm

Blue Earth Books
an imprint of Capstone Press

Blue Earth Books
818 North Willow Street, Mankato, Minnesota 56001
http://www.capstone-press.com

Library of Congress Cataloging-in-Publication Data
O'Hara, Megan.
    Pioneer farm: living on a farm in the 1880s/by Megan O'Hara.
    p. cm.--(Living history)
    Includes bibliographical references (p. 30) and index.
    Summary: Uses the story of a young girl and her family to describe life on a small farm in
Minnesota in the nineteenth century.
    ISBN 1-56065-726-X
    1. Agriculture--Minnesota--History--Juvenile literature. 2. Farm life--Minnesota--History--
Juvenile literature. 3. Frontier and pioneer life--Minnesota--Juvenile literature. [1. Farm life--
Minnesota. 2. Frontier and pioneer life--Minnesota. 3. Minnesota--History--1858-] I. Title. II.
Series: Living history (Mankato, Minn.)
S519.034 1998
630'.978'09034--dc21   97-31874
                                                     CIP
                                                     AC

Editorial credits:

Editor, Christy Steele; design, Patricia Bickner Linder; illustrations, Timothy Halldin

Photo credits:

All photography by Tim Rummelhoff

Contents

Acknowledgments

We are grateful to the following for contributing their time, knowledge, and expertise: Jim Mattson, site manager, Oliver Kelley Farm; Laurie Brickley and Liz Turchin of the Minnesota Historical Society; interpreters and volunteers Michaela Bercher, Ann Olson Bercher, John Gutteter, Shalene Rooney, and Reed Heidelberger. We are also grateful for the use of this Minnesota Historical Society site and artifacts to recreate life at a pioneer farm.

**Location of the Oliver Kelley Farm
Elk River, Minnesota**

Introduction

Pioneer farmers grew, raised, or made most of the supplies they needed. They grew vegetables and fruits in their gardens. They raised horses to help them with farm work. They raised chickens, pigs, cattle, and sheep for meat, milk, and wool. They made their own clothes and churned their own butter. They could trade some of their goods and foods for tools and supplies they did not have.

Farmers worked outdoors most of the time in spring, summer, and fall. They plowed fields and planted seeds. They cared for crops and livestock.

Women and children did indoor tasks as well as working in the garden and pastures. Each day had its own set of chores. A popular saying in the 1800s lists daily chores:

Wash on Monday,
Iron on Tuesday,
Mend on Wednesday,
Churn on Thursday,
Clean on Friday,
Bake on Saturday,
Rest on Sunday.

Children were important on 19th-century farms. They carried pails of water into the house. Outside wells supplied water. Children also fed and watched farm animals. They helped their families by cleaning, churning butter, and bringing in wood and kindling for baking. They worked in gardens, too.

Grace and her family are fictional characters. But their story is based on the real stories of farm families who lived in Minnesota during the 1880s. These real families left letters and diaries for others to read. They lived on farms like the Oliver Kelley Farm in Elk River, Minnesota.

Getting Up and Getting Dressed

Our mother calls us to get ready for the day. There are many chores to do. My name is Grace. I live here on our family farm with my mother, father, and older sister, Clara. It is often dark outside when Clara and I rise. It is now harvest season. During harvest, we gather the crops we have grown. It is hard work. This morning there is a little light to stir us from our sleep.

We wear our everyday dresses and put pinafores over them. Our pinafores are like aprons. They keep our dresses clean.

After breakfast we start our chores for the day. We always wear sunbonnets when we work outdoors. I sometimes take my bonnet off so I can feel the warm sun on my face.

Feeding the Animals

One of our first chores is feeding grain to the chickens. We also gather eggs from the chicken house. The hens try to peck our hands when we remove their eggs. The eggs feel warm, even on cold days.

Next, we feed the pigs. They are always hungry and snorting. My sister and I call them by yelling "sooey." The pigs run to eat the grain and table scraps we bring them. This year we have a lot of watermelon, so we feed some to the pigs. They seem to like it. Pigs seem to like everything.

Every morning, we stop to see how the sheep are doing. The lambs were born in the spring. Now they are covered with thick fleece. They look like they will provide a lot of wool. Mother will use the wool to make new clothes for us.

Making Wool into Clothes

Once a year, pioneer farmers sheared their sheep. To shear means to cut the fleece off a sheep. Fleece is a coat of tangled wool fibers.

By the 1880s, farmers sold the fleeces. But in early pioneer days, women spun the wool themselves. To make fleece into wool, they first picked the twigs and burrs out of the curly fleece. Then they combed the curly wool to untangle the fibers.

After combing, the women spun the wool fibers. Spinning is twisting the wool fibers into yarn.

Women made clothes out of the yarn. When families had extra yarn, they traded it for food and other goods.

Wash Day

We still have regular chores to do during harvest time. Today is wash day. Mother needs our help. We pump and haul water. I do not like this chore. The buckets of water are so heavy!

Before we wash clothes, we must heat the water in a big copper tub set on top of the woodstove.

On nice days like this, we do the washing outside. We set up two tubs. The first tub holds water, soap, and the washboard. Mother rubs the clothes up and down against the washboard. This gets the dirt out.

The second tub holds rinse water. Clara and I rinse the clothes. We make sure all the soap comes out of the fabric.

Then we pull the clothes through the wringer. It squeezes out all the water. Wringing is hard work, but it helps the clothes dry faster.

We hang the clothes outside to dry. The weather today is perfect for drying the wash. The air is dry, and there is a soft breeze.

Tomorrow will be ironing day.

Threshing Season

Father and the neighbors are working hard to thresh our grain. Sometimes Father pays hired hands to help him thresh.

Threshing is a big task. First, they take bundles of grain such as wheat or oats from stacks in and around the barn. Then they feed the bundles into the noisy threshing machine. The machine threshes the grain and separates it from the chaff and the straw. Then they measure the grain and put it into bags.

We store the grain in the granary or sell it in town. We stack the straw in and around the barn. We use it as bedding in the livestock stalls and pens. The straw keeps the animals warm and clean.

Our neighbors have a steam-powered thresher. Father says our old horse-powered thresher works just as well. Horses do not break down as machines sometimes do.

Dinner

Mother, Clara, and I prepare dinner after we finish washing. We slice fresh bread and cheese. We cook vegetables and a chicken. There is barely enough time in the morning to get everything done.

We sometimes have a crew helping during the threshing season. At noon, everyone takes a break from threshing and chores. It is time for dinner. This is the biggest meal of the day.

Gardening

We work in the garden in the afternoon. It is one of our most important tasks.

Clara and I pull out the weeds. We do not want the weeds to crowd out the good plants. My hands are sore after weeding. Sometimes my back hurts, too.

We gather the vegetables and fruit when they are ripe. Today, there are many tomatoes, squash, melons, and cabbages to pick.

Our garden produces more food than we can eat right away. But we do not want to waste anything. We pickle, can, and store the vegetables and fruit. We store the potatoes, carrots, and turnips in bins of sand in our root cellar. We dry the onions and hang them from a nail. We will eat these foods all winter long.

Grow Your Own Beans

What You Need

Two or three green bean seeds
A small pot
Planting soil

What You Do

1. Fill one-half of the pot with soil.
2. Place the bean seeds on the soil.
3. Fill the rest of the pot with soil.
4. Sprinkle a little water on the soil.
5. Put the pot in a sunny place.
6. Water the soil once a week.

You can watch the beans grow. In six to eight weeks, you can pick the beans.

We are picking the last of our tomatoes. We will stew and can some for the winter. Mother will also make ketchup from tomatoes. Ketchup is delicious.

Preparing for Winter

Beans, beans, beans. There are so many beans to shell and sort. We shell the beans by taking off their hard outer coverings. Then we put the beans in large bags.

We hang the bags in a dry place in the barn to keep the beans from spoiling. These beans will last us all winter. Mother will bake them or put them in soup.

Churning

Churning butter is another one of our jobs. We make sure the butter churn is clean before we begin. Mother says otherwise our butter will taste bad.

To make butter, we use cream from the cows' milk. We let the milk set for a day, and then we skim cream off the top. I put the cream in the churn. The churn has a special handle called a dasher. The dasher is a pole with a wooden disk on the end. The disk has holes in it to churn the cream.

My arms and shoulders ache from pushing the dasher up and down. Sometimes Clara and I take turns. It takes about 30 minutes of churning to make butter. Churning separates the cream into butter and buttermilk.

There are round bits of butter in the churn. I scoop the butter into wooden bowls and wash it carefully with water. This removes the buttermilk. Buttermilk makes butter spoil. Mother will use the buttermilk for baking or as a healthy drink.

I use wooden paddles to work the butter until it is smooth. Then I stir in a little salt. Salt flavors the butter and keeps it from spoiling. We will sell some of the butter and store the rest in a cool place.

Churn Your Own Butter

What You Need
One cup of whipping cream
One bowl
One small glass jar with a lid
One wooden spoon
Cold water
Salt

What You Do
1. Put the whipping cream into the jar. Put the lid on the jar.
2. Shake the jar for 30 minutes. Watch the cream separate as you shake it. The butter is the yellow bits. The buttermilk is the liquid.
3. Pour the contents of the jar into a bowl.
4. Pour the buttermilk down a sink drain.
5. Pour a little cold water over the butter to rinse off the buttermilk. Push the butter against the side of the bowl with the wooden spoon as you rinse it. This will remove all of the buttermilk.
6. Stir in a little salt.
7. Butter a slice of bread and eat it.
8. Store the rest of your butter in the refrigerator.

Make an Apple Fruit Cake

This is an old-time recipe for apple fruit cake. Baking was less exact 100 years ago. People measured with ordinary teacups and spoons. But this fruit cake can be made using modern methods. Ask an adult to help you with the recipe.

What You Need

1 cup (.24 liter) of butter
3 cups (.72 liter) of dried apples
2 eggs
1 teaspoon (5 milliliters) of baking soda
3-1/2 cups (.84 liter) of flour
1 cup (.24 liter) of milk
2 cups (.48 liter) of molasses
2 cups (.48 liter) of sugar
2 cups (.48 liter) of raisins
13 by 9 inch (33 by 23 centimeters) cake pan

What You Do

1. Soak the dried apples in a bowl of water overnight. Cut the soaked apples into small pieces.
2. Put the apples and molasses in a pot. Put the pot on the stove. Cook the mixture slowly over low heat for two hours.
3. Preheat the oven to 350 degrees Fahrenheit (177 degrees Celsius).
4. Put butter and sugar into a bowl. Beat the mixture until it is creamy.
5. Put the baking soda and milk into a larger bowl. Stir the baking soda into the milk until the baking soda dissolves.
6. Add the butter and sugar mixture to the milk mixture. This is the batter for the cake.
7. Put the eggs into a small bowl. Beat the eggs with a fork.
8. Add the eggs and the flour to the batter. Mix the batter well.
9. Add the raisins and the stewed apples to the batter. Mix it well.
10. Butter the cake pan. Sprinkle flour over the butter.
11. Pour the batter into the pan.
12. Put the pan in the oven. Bake for 90 minutes.
13. Let the fruit cake cool for one hour before eating it.

From *The Buckeye Cookery and Practical Housekeeping* edited by Estelle Woods Wilcox

Husking and Baking

Tomorrow our family is going to a cornhusking bee. All of our neighbors will be there, too. We will take the outer casings off ears of corn. This is husking. Each of us will husk hundreds of ears of corn.

Today Mother, Clara, and I are baking an apple cake. We will bring it to the cornhusking bee. We cook with dried apples from last year's apple harvest. A summer hailstorm destroyed this year's apples.

We always have a big party after the husking bee. Each family brings good food to eat. After eating, we dance to fiddle music and play games. My friends and I sometimes make dolls out of corn husks.

Make a Corn Husk Doll

What You Need

Seven or more dried corn husks
String
Scissors

What You Do

1. Tie the narrow ends of six corn husks together with a piece of string.
2. Fold the broad ends of the husks back over the tied area.
3. Tie string around the husks about one inch (2.54 centimeters) from the top. This will make the head and neck.
4. Roll a corn husk into a tube for the arms.
5. Slide the arms between the husks and under the head.
6. Tie another string under the arms for the waist.
7. Use the scissors to trim the loose ends of the husks. This will make a skirt.
8. You can tie other husks to the doll to make a hat, a scarf, a shawl, or an apron.

Step One

Step Two

Step Three

Step Four

Step Five

Step Six

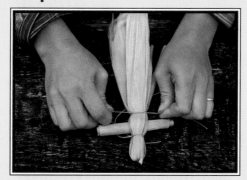

Step Seven

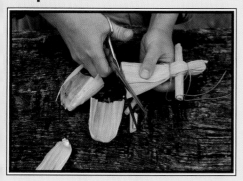

Step Eight

Watching Cows

Clara and I like to play games while we watch the cows. We often clap to our favorite rhymes. In winter, we play Fox and Geese.

Play Fox and Geese

What You Do
1. Walk a big circle into the snow at least 50 feet (15 meters) wide.
2. Make eight lines running through the circle. The circle should look like a pie cut into pieces.
3. Make a small circle in the middle of the larger circle.
4. Choose one person to be the fox. The rest of the players are the geese.
5. Tell the fox to chase the geese around the circle and up and down the lines. Geese are free if they reach the small circle in the center. When a goose is tagged, the goose becomes the fox.

Evening Hours

Clara and I play together after we have eaten supper and cleaned the dishes. Sometimes Mother lets us play with her china doll. She brought it with her from Germany when she was a child. But usually Clara and I play with our corn husk dolls.

Harvest days on the farm are long and hard. But we all work together. Our work gives us food to eat and clothes to wear.

Words to Know

churn (CHURN)—a container in which cream is made into butter

dasher (DASH-ur)—a pole with a wooden disk on the end that is used to make butter

harvest season (HAR-vist SEE-zuhn)—the time of year when ripe crops are picked and gathered; between July and October

husking (HUHSK-ing)—removing the outer casing of seeds, vegetables, or grains

pickle (PIK-uhl)—to preserve food in vinegar or salt water

pinafore (PIN-ah-for)—an outer covering for a dress

plow (PLOW)—to prepare soil for planting seeds

sunbonnet (SUHN-bon-it)—a hat used to protect the face from the sun

threshing (THRESH-ing)—separating the grain from a plant's stem

To Learn More

Bial, **Raymond**. *Frontier Home*. Boston: Houghton Mifflin, 1993.

Greenwood, **Barbara**. *A Pioneer Sampler: The Daily Life of a Pioneer Family in 1840*. New York: Ticknor & Fields Books for Young Readers, 1995.

Kalman, **Bobbi**. *In the Barn*. New York: Crabtree Publishing, 1997.

Internet Sites

ALHFAM Links
http://www.mysticseaport.org/alhfam/alhfam.links.html

Conner Prairie
http://www.connerprairie.org/cp

Living History Domain
http://livinghistory.com/index.html

Minnesota Historical Society
http://www.mnhs.org/index.html

Places to Write and Visit

California
Monterey County Agricultural and Rural Life Museum
1160 Broadway
King City, CA 93930

Colorado
Four Mile Historic Park
715 S. Forest Street
Denver, CO 80222

Georgia
Shields-Ethridge Heritage Farm
P.O. Box 662
Jefferson, GA 30549

Illinois
Garfield Farm Museum
P.O. Box 403
LaFox, IL 60147

Kline Creek Farm
Timber Ridge Forest Preserve
County Farm Road
Winfield, IL 60190

Naper Settlement
523 South Webster Street
Naperville, IL 60540

Indiana
Conner Prairie
13400 Allisonville Road
Fishers, IN 46038-4499

Iowa
Living History Farms
2600 NW 111th Street
Urbandale, IA 50322

Massachusetts
Freeman Farm
Old Sturbridge Village
1 Old Sturbridge Village Rd.
Sturbridge, MA 01566

Hancock Shaker Village
P.O. Box 927
Pittsfield, MA 01202

Michigan
Cobblestone Farm Museum
2781 Packard Road
Ann Arbor, MI 48103

Minnesota
Oliver Kelley Farm
15788 Kelley Farm Road
Elk River, MN 55330

New Jersey
Howell Living History Farm
101 Hunter Road
Titusville, NJ 08560

Ohio
Hale Farm and Village
P.O. Box 296
Bath, OH 44210

Pennsylvania
Landis Valley Museum
2451 Kissel Hill Road
Lancaster, PA 17601

Peter Wentz Farmstead
P.O. Box 240
Worcester, PA 19490

Texas
Farmstead Museum
P.O. Box 157
Pittsburg, TX 75686

Penn Farm
Cedar Hill State Park
P.O. Box 2649
Cedar Hill, TX 75104

Sauer-Beckmann Living History Farm
Lyndon B. Johnson State Historical Park
P.O. Box 238
Stonewall, TX 78671

Virginia
George Ranch Historical Park
P.O. Box 1248
Richmond, VA 77406

Ottawa, Canada
Agriculture Museum
P.O. Box 9724, Station T
Ottawa, ON K1G 5A3
Canada

31

About the Oliver Kelley Farm

The Oliver Kelley Farm is a 189-acre (75.6-hectare) living history farm located on the Mississippi River in Elk River, Minnesota. It is owned and operated by the Minnesota Historical Society and is open to the public from May through October.

Interpreters perform the tasks of Minnesota farm families in the mid-nineteenth century. Interpreters wear clothing of that time period as they teach visitors and school children about Minnesota's agricultural history.

During the different seasons of farm work, visitors might see horse-powered threshing, reaping with a McCormick daisy self-raking reaper, or plowing with a team of oxen. Heirloom varieties of crops and vegetables from the farm's collection grow in the gardens and fields. Historic breeds of draft animals work the fields. Visitors can see livestock bred to exhibit historic characteristics in the pasture or farm pens. Visitors can also learn about domestic crafts such as cooking or making soap.

For more information, call the Minnesota Historical Society at 612-441-6896 or visit the society's Internet site at <http://www.mnhs.org>.